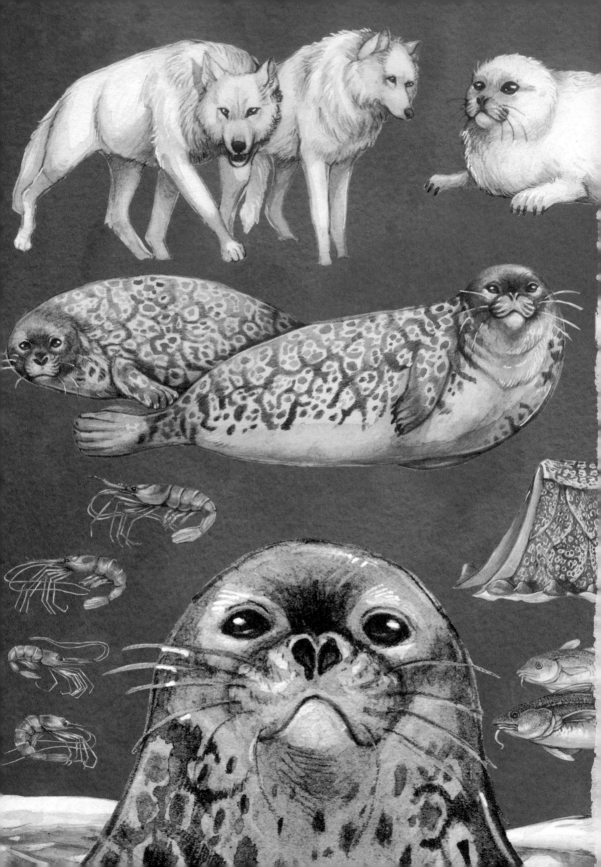

·ANIMALS ILLUSTRATED·

Ringed Seal

· ANIMALS ILLUSTRATED ·

Ringed Seal

by William Flaherty • illustrated by Sara Otterstätter

INHABIT
MEDIA

Note to readers: For Inuktitut-language resources, including pronunciation assistance for Inuktitut terms found in this book, please visit inhabitmedia.com/inuitnipingit.

Published by Inhabit Media Inc.
www.inhabitmedia.com

Inhabit Media Inc. (Iqaluit) P.O. Box 11125, Iqaluit, Nunavut, X0A 1H0

Design and layout copyright © 2022 Inhabit Media Inc.
Text copyright © 2022 by William Flaherty
Illustrations by Sara Otterstätter copyright © 2022 Inhabit Media Inc.

Editors: Neil Christopher and Kelly Ward
Art Directors: Danny Christopher and Astrid Arijanto

We acknowledge the support of the Canada Council for the Arts for our publishing program.

This project was made possible in part by the Government of Canada.

ISBN: 978-1-77227-370-0

Printed in Canada

Library and Archives Canada Cataloguing in Publication

Title: Ringed seal / by William Flaherty ; illustrated by Sara Otterstätter.
Names: Flaherty, William, 1965- author. | Otterstätter, Sara, 1978- illustrator.
Series: Animals illustrated.
Description: Series statement: Animals illustrated
Identifiers: Canadiana 20220167222 | ISBN 9781772273700 (hardcover)
Subjects: LCSH: Ringed seal—Juvenile literature.
Classification: LCC QL737.P64 F53 2022 | DDC j599.79/2—dc23

Table of Contents

2   The Ringed Seal

4   Range

6   Skeleton

8   Claws

10   Blubber

12   Diet

14   Babies

16   Predators

18   Intelligence

20   Traditional Uses

The Ringed Seal

Ringed seals live in the oceans of the circumpolar North, meaning the area at the top of the globe, including Canada's Arctic. Ringed seal fur is darker on the animal's back, and lighter on its underside. Ringed seals also have light rings in the fur on their backs, which is where their name comes from. The dark, patterned fur allows the seals to blend in with the dark ocean water when viewed by predators from above.

Ringed seals are the most common seals found in Nunavut. They are the smallest species of seal found in the Arctic. Ringed seals can grow up to 5 feet (about 1.5 metres) in length and weigh up to 150 pounds (about 68 kilograms).

Let's learn more about ringed seals!

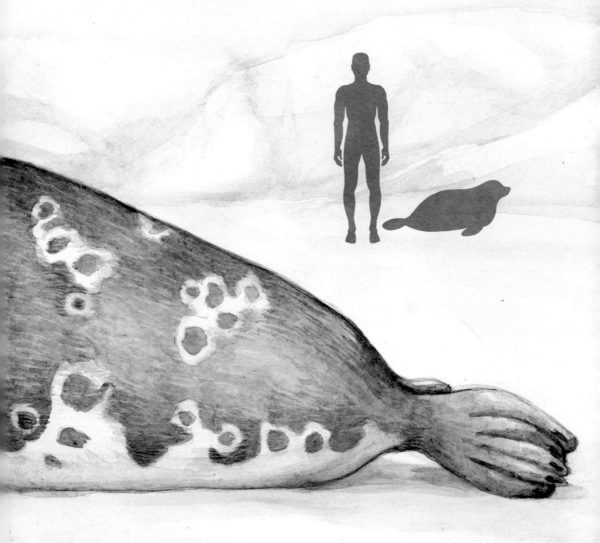

Range

Ringed seals are found all over the northern parts of the globe, including the Canadian Arctic, Alaska, Greenland, and Arctic Europe. Ringed seals like to spend most of their time on the ice and in the ocean. They rarely bask on the shoreline, though it is becoming more common to see them on the shore. They usually live alone, only coming together in a group to mate.

Ringed seals stay in Arctic waters all year long. The farther north you go in the Arctic, the more ringed seals there are. Ringed seals from the more northern parts of their range tend to be bigger than those from the southern part of their range.

Skeleton

Skull

Scapula

Phalanges ——

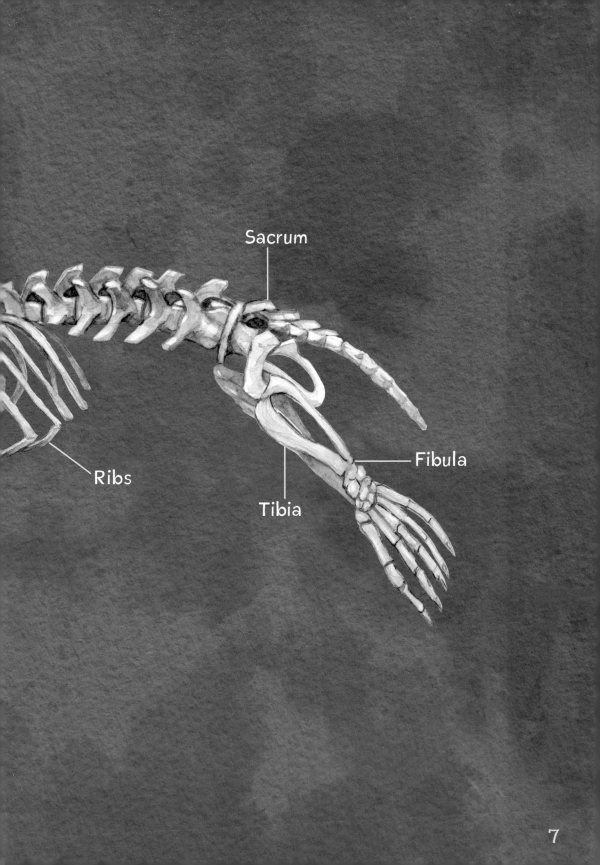

Sacrum

Ribs

Fibula

Tibia

Claws

Ringed seals are excellent diggers! They use the strong, thick claws on their front flippers to make holes in the ice so they can breathe. As the ice forms in the fall, ringed seals dig to keep breathing holes open, making sure the holes remain clear as the ice thickens.

Flippers

Once a ringed seal has dug a breathing hole, it will keep the hole from freezing by surfacing in the hole regularly to breathe. The splashing of the seal in the hole creates a thin frozen roof over the hole, which looks like a cone when seen on the ice.

Breathing hole

Blubber

Like other marine mammals, ringed seals are covered in a thick layer of fat called "blubber." Blubber helps keep ringed seals warm in the cold water of the Arctic Ocean. Blubber also stores fats and proteins that ringed seals need to survive. If a ringed seal can't find food to eat, it can live off the fats and proteins stored in its blubber. Blubber also helps ringed seals float in the water.

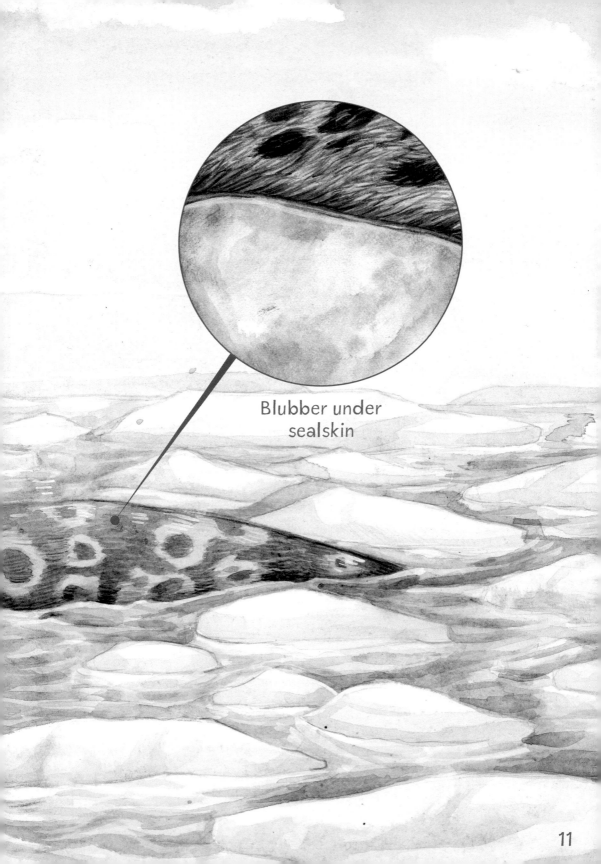

Blubber under
sealskin

Diet

Ringed seals are meat eaters and dive to catch their food. They eat cod, shrimp, and other types of fish and tiny sea animals.

Ringed seals can dive deep into the ocean to find food, as far as 150 feet down (about 46 metres). They can stay underwater for up to 20 minutes before needing to breathe.

Cod

Shrimp

Babies

Baby ringed seals are called "pups." In Nunavut they are born in the winter months, January to April. Usually only one pup is born at a time.

Ringed seal pups are born in a birthing lair or den on the ice. After selecting a good mound of snow near rough ice, the mother seal creates a hollow dome in the snow.

There is a hole in the ice below so she can continue to dive for food.

A pup stays in the den with its mother for about two months. During that time, it drinks milk from its mother and learns to dive soon after birth. After a couple of months, the pup no longer needs its mother's milk and it can live on its own.

Predators

Ringed seals are an important food for lots of animals in the Arctic, including humans. Ringed seals are eaten by people all over the Arctic and hunted at their breathing holes.

Polar bear

Arctic wolves

Like humans, polar bears can hunt ringed seals at their breathing holes, thrusting their heads into the hole to catch a seal. Wolves can also hunt them on the ice. Arctic foxes dig into seals' birthing lairs to prey on small pups.

Arctic fox

Intelligence

Ringed seals don't have many ways to protect themselves from predators, but ringed seals are not easy to catch! Hunters know them to be quite smart and good at staying away from danger.

Hunters must use a hunting blind—a white sheet that helps a hunter blend in with the sea ice—when hunting ringed seals that are basking on the sea ice in the spring, or the seals will notice them and get away before being caught.

In the wintertime, ringed seals will even send bubbles up to the surface before actually surfacing to breathe to see if a predator is waiting above.

Traditional Uses

Because ringed seals are the most common seals found in Nunavut, Inuit have a lot of uses for them!

Seal stew

Ringed seal meat can be eaten raw, fried, or boiled with vegetables and seasonings. The flippers are especially tasty when aged or boiled.

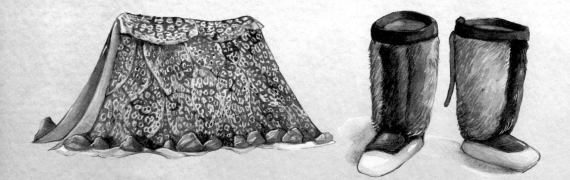

Sealskin tent   Sealskin boots

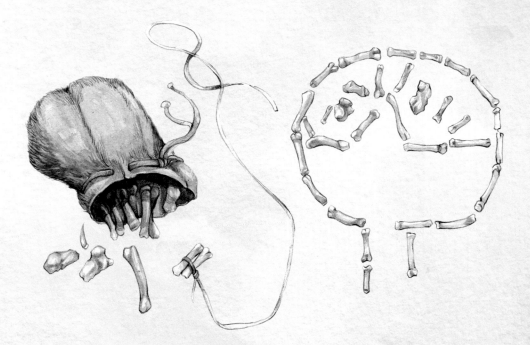

Seal bone games

Ringed seal bones were traditionally used for children's toys and games. Flipper bones would be put into a bag (sometimes an old mitt) and fished out with a noose. Then the children would compete to make a toy sod house from the bones they had caught. There was also a game using two bones attached by a string. Children would try to catch the hole of the larger bone with the smaller bone.

Ringed seal skin was traditionally used to make clothing, boots, tents, water buckets, packs for dogs, and many other things. Ringed seal clothing was worn throughout the year, but especially in summer and fall, as it was not as thick as caribou-skin clothing.

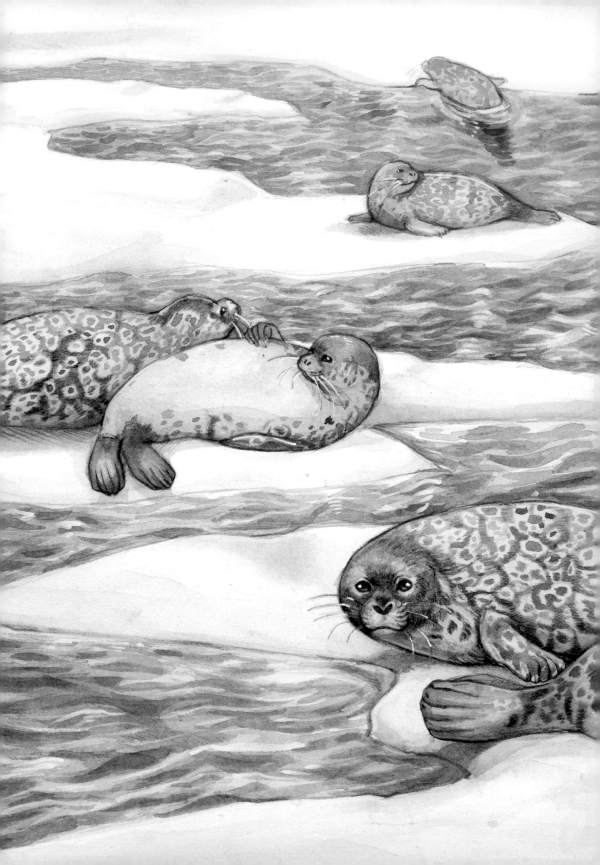

William Flaherty is a conservation officer in Iqaluit, Nunavut. He is a graduate from the Environmental Studies Program of Nunavut Arctic College. William has been part of the Iqaluit Search and Rescue team for many years. William is also a graduate of the Carpentry Program of Thebatcha College, Fort Smith, Northwest Territories.

Sara Otterstätter studied illustration and graphic design at the University for Applied Studies in Münster, Germany. Since 2007 she has been working as a freelance illustrator for German and international publishing houses. The focus of her works is educational illustrations for children.

www.inhabitmedia.com